HAL LEONARD
GUITAR METHOD

BLUES GUITAR
BY GREG KOCH

PLAYBACK+
Speed • Pitch • Balance • Loop

To access audio visit:
www.halleonard.com/mylibrary

Enter Code
8128-9457-1707-6335

ISBN 978-0-634-03389-6

HAL•LEONARD®

Visit Hal Leonard Online at
www.halleonard.com

Contact us:
Hal Leonard
7777 West Bluemound Road
Milwaukee, WI 53213
Email: info@halleonard.com

In Europe, contact:
Hal Leonard Europe Limited
42 Wigmore Street
Marylebone, London, W1U 2RN
Email: info@halleonardeurope.com

In Australia, contact:
Hal Leonard Australia Pty. Ltd.
4 Lentara Court
Cheltenham, Victoria, 3192 Australia
Email: info@halleonard.com.au

CONTENTS

INTRODUCTION

Welcome to the Hal Leonard Blues Guitar method. The goal of this book is to teach the basic elements of blues guitar while using simple yet authentic arrangements of true blues classics. As you wind your way through this book, the development of your blues technique will include a variety of rhythm studies including movable patterns, turnarounds, and stylistically correct chord shapes. Lead blues guitar will be introduced from the beginning, starting with the blues scale and adding blues nuances such as slides, bends, pull-offs, hammer-ons, vibrato, and double stops along the way. While working through the songs of Robert Johnson, B.B. King, Albert King, Freddie King, T-Bone Walker, Muddy Waters, Stevie Ray Vaughan, and others, you will acquire the basic skills necessary to head out to a blues jam or fire up a jam in the basement with some friends.

GUITARS AND AMPS

This book was written with the electric guitar in mind, but if armed with only an acoustic, you will still be able to work your way through most of the examples, especially if you use an unwound G string for easier bending. It's a good idea to take a minute to address what kind of electric guitars and amplifiers are the most "blues friendly."

In choosing an electric guitar to best facilitate playing the blues, you may want to consider what artists you admire and what they use to get their tone. There are differing schools of thought on guitar tone, and that does reflect in how one approaches the instrument. For instance, the beefy tone of humbucker pickups found on such guitars as the Gibson ES-335, Les Paul, Flying V, and SG, the Guild Starfire and Bluesbird, among others, are distinctive in the more singing, lead accompaniment styles of artists such as B.B., Albert, and Freddie King; whereas the glassy, brighter tone of single-coil pickups found in Fender Stratocasters, Telecasters, and Danelectro guitars, among others, are key in the more rhythmic, biting styles of players such as Muddy Waters, Buddy Guy, and Stevie Ray Vaughan. The actual playability of these instruments is as much a matter of taste as the tone. I suggest testing out a variety of guitars and find something you are comfortable with as well as one you look forward to playing.

As for amplification, you'll find a warm, meaty, articulate tone using an old Fender, Gibson, or National tube amp. These were the chosen "tone consoles" for many of the blues greats. More contemporary blues artists who may demand more distortion might lean towards modern Fender, Marshall, MESA, Sunn, or any variety of high-gain amps. Although solid-state technology was panned for years as being sterile and harsh, a number of manufacturers have come up with some pretty believable and affordable models. Again, I would consider the tones of some of your favorite artists: Stevie Ray Vaughan used Fender Super Reverbs predominately, B.B. King opted for the Fender Twin, John Mayall- and Cream-era Eric Clapton preferred Marshalls. In the end, whatever makes sense to you in terms of sound, size, and price is good to go!

Gibson ES-175 (left), Gibson ES-335 (right) and tweed 4x10 Fender Bassman combo amp

Fender Stratocasters and 4x12 Marshall stack

PICK VS. FINGERS

One of the many great things about playing blues guitar is that there are no rules. Many a great bluesman, from Albert King to Albert Collins, have forsaken the plectrum in favor of flesh on string. I tend to steer people toward experimenting with both so that you can get the best of both worlds. How you attack the strings can make a huge difference in the sound, and ultimately, the way you express yourself. A pick is going to give you a brighter, more aggressive sound, and a fingerstyle attack gives a mellower touch that can be made more aggressive by popping the strings. Again, experiment with both!

STANDING VS. SITTING

Another habit that I encourage in order to prepare for eventually performing out in public or with friends is that you stand when you practice. This doesn't mean you need to stand every time you grab the guitar, but once you've got a new lick or technique "under your fingers," put a strap on and get used to playing it while standing. The way you distribute your weight, how you approach the guitar, and the difference in how you support the instrument will all make a big difference in how well you play when standing versus sitting.

And while you're at it, plug in. In the the same way that the difference between sitting and standing can be night and day, practicing unplugged with an electric guitar can make for an eye-opening experience when you finally do get powered up. How you dampen strings, dynamics, and overall tone can be grossly misjudged if not amplified, so be sure you spend enough time plugged in if you're playing an electric guitar.

HAND POSITIONING

When you see blues guitarists in action, you'll notice that their thumbs are often wrapped around the neck as opposed to the more traditional grip, which has the thumb located on the back of the neck to facilitate a "piston-like" action by your fingers on the fretboard. The reason for this is that it gives you extra leverage for bending notes. It is important, however, to be able to go back and forth between these hand positions as your technique develops, but for the purposes of this book, it will be easier to do the bending exercises with the "thumb over the neck" hand positioning.

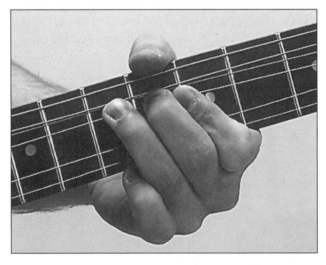

Thumb positioning for playing blues

THE 12-BAR BLUES

The blues is a musical form as much as it is a musical style or feeling. The most common blues form is the **12-bar blues** consisting of the I–IV–V progression. And the language can be further embellished with terms such as "dominant seventh chord," "quick change," or "turnaround." As you might have guessed, most of these terms have their roots in music theory, though they should not send the would-be blues enthusiast into pangs of terror. I'll try to make it simple so as not to give you the blues!

The progression below is a blues in the key of G. It consists of twelve measures, or bars, and the chords within this blues form are the I (G7), IV (C7), and V (D7) chords in the key of G. This would be an example of a "quick change," because after the first bar of the I chord (G7), the harmony shifts immediately to the IV chord (C7). The last two bars are known as the "turnaround" because chordally, it turns you around to the I chord at the top of the progression.

TRACK 1

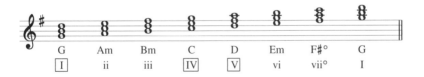

The chords that are predominately used in the blues are dominant seventh chords. The following figures go a long way in explaining where I, IV, V and dominant seventh terminology comes from. If you build chords by stacking 3rds above each scale degree in the G major scale and put a Roman numeral under each one as you count away from the root note (G), you'll find a series of seven chords. The I, IV, and V chords (G, C, and D) are the basic chord components for the blues form.

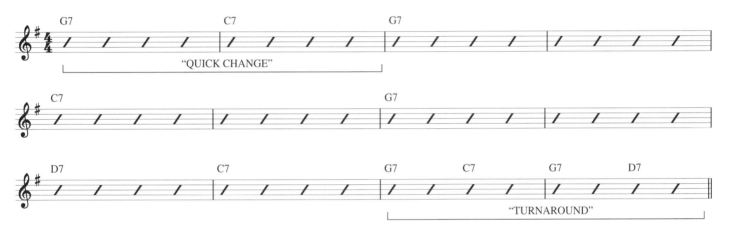

In the figure below, you'll see that if you add another note on top of the triads, making them seventh chords, the V chord or dominant chord as it is also called, is a major triad with a flatted or minor seventh. The sound of that chord is widely used in blues and jazz and musicians use the term dominant seventh to differentiate this chord from the more "happy-sounding" major seventh chord, which is a major triad with a major seventh added to it. The words tonic, mediant, dominant, etc. were terms used in addition to the Roman numerals by music theorists to explain and describe the relationships of notes and chords in a scale. These chordal relationships are the same in every major key. The names of the notes change but the relationships are the same.

THE SHUFFLE RHYTHM

Many blues songs use a rhythmic feel called the **shuffle**. In this rhythm, eighth notes are played unevenly; the first note is twice as long as the second.

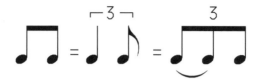

The shuffle rhythm can be played fast or slow. Listen to the tracks to hear how the following examples sound. Then, play along when you are ready. Once you get the hang of this "bouncy" feel, you will never forget it.

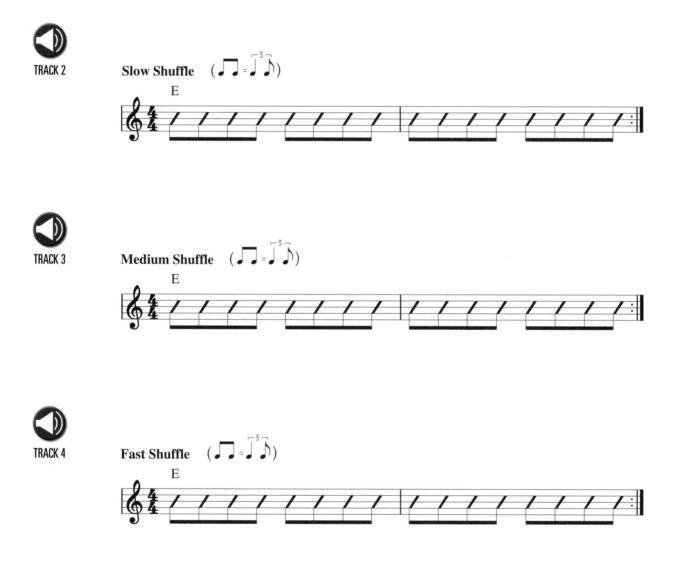

"Sweet Home Chicago" was written by Robert Johnson and has been performed by Magic Sam, the Blues Brothers, and virtually every blues band in the world at one time or another. It is a classic blues shuffle in the key of E, and this particular arrangement starts with a chordal turnaround as the introduction, which is more often than not the case with blues tunes. As this book progresses, you will acquire an arsenal of turnarounds, but this is a good one with which to start.

TRACK 5

SWEET HOME CHICAGO

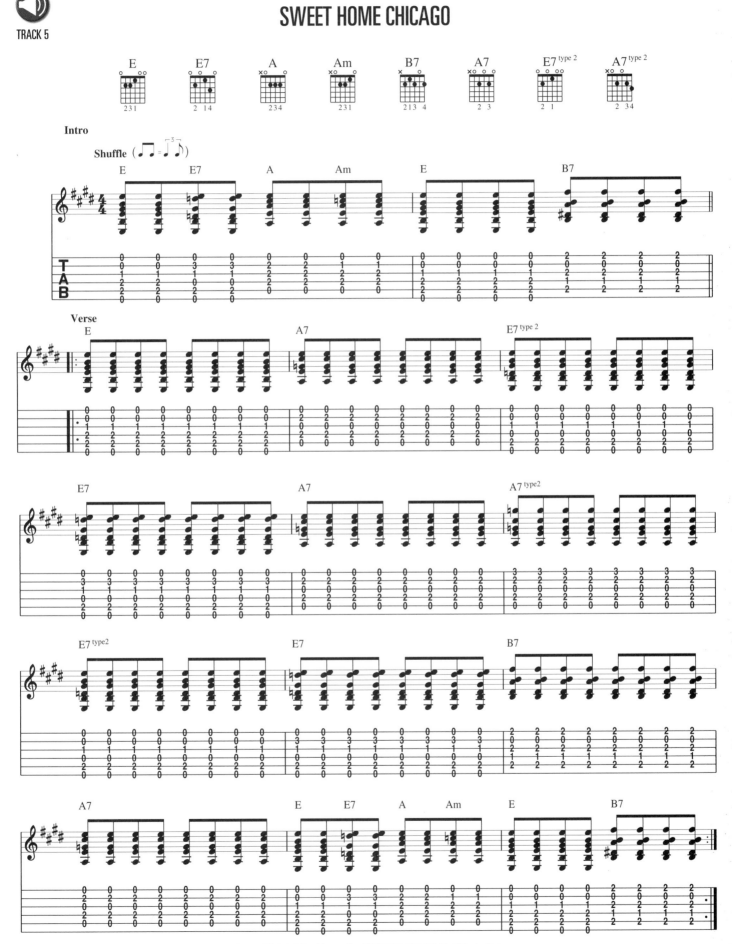

THE BLUES SCALE

The most commonly used scale in blues music is (you guessed it!) the **blues scale**. The blues scale is a six-note scale that contains the root, ♭3rd, 4th, 5th, ♭5th, and ♭7th (or "blue note"). In using these notes you can successfully improvise over each chord of a typical twelve bar blues in that key. Here is the E blues scale in open position.

The E Blues Scale

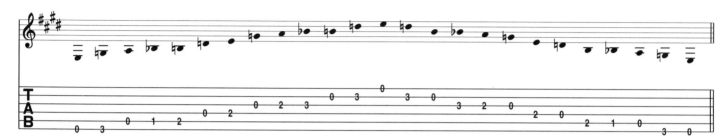

Getting the sound of the blues scale ingrained in your brain as soon as possible will go a long way in enabling you to solo or improvise over a blues tune. Below is an exercise using the E blues scale in first position over the verse chords of "Sweet Home Chicago." It is a good example of how the notes of the blues scale work over all the chords of a blues. Playing blues guitar initially can be made easier by visual association on the guitar neck. I want you to make the visual connection between this scale "box" position and this blues progression which has its root note based on the E string on your guitar. This visual connection will help immensely as we start moving the E string based blues tunes up the neck.

TRACK 6

Try playing the above example again, playing each note twice with the shuffle rhythm.

The Rolling Stones covered Robert Johnson's "Love in Vain Blues" on their *Let It Bleed* record, and it is a good example of a G blues in open position. Note the new chordal turnaround in the intro as it is a classic "country blues" example. This arrangement also employs the shuffle rhythm. Try to mute the root notes of the chords with your palm of your right hand while letting the higher strings ring out.

TRACK 7

LOVE IN VAIN BLUES

BLUES PHRASING

The organization and delivery of notes in a solo is often called **phrasing**. Learn the following scale, then practice playing the solo phrases in the example at the bottom of the page.

The G blues scale in open position can be used to solo over this particular arrangement. The example written here starts and ends with the root note to help you visually associate it with the chord positions. Most blues "fills" or "runs" are based around the root note of the blues progression so it is always good to get your bearings, in any position of the blues scale, around the root.

The G Blues Scale

The following phrasing example uses triplets while soloing around the root note of each chord. All of the notes are derived from the G blues scale. Using triplets when soloing can go a long way in helping your phrasing sound bluesy.

Now, play along with the next example remembering the shuffle rhythm when playing the eighth notes. Then try your own blues phrasing while soloing over the verse chords of "Love in Vain Blues."

TRACK 8

Once again, a Robert Johnson composition strikes, this time as an arrangement derived from the version of "From Four Until Late" that Eric Clapton did in 1967 with the supergroup Cream on their debut release *Fresh Cream*. It includes yet another chordal turnaround as the intro and a root/5th bass pattern steeped in the country blues tradition. Note that this blues also includes a VI–II chord sequence (A7–D7) sometimes added to the standard blues progression to add a little flavor.

FROM FOUR UNTIL LATE

Words and Music by Robert Johnson   Copyright © (1978), 1990, 1991 King Of Spades Music
All Rights Reserved   Used by Permission

After playing along with the chords of "From Four Until Late," try improvising with the C blues scale. The C blues scale in first position is not as common as some of the other box positions but is useful nonetheless. I have started the scale on the root going up then down then back up ending on the beginning root note just to make it a little more musical. As you did with the G blues scale in "Love in Vain Blues," try to visualize the C blues scale in relation to the chords in "From Four Until Late."

The C Blues Scale

STRING BENDING

An important technique for playing blues guitar is **bending** strings. This technique produces the characteristic moaning or "singing-like" sound of blues guitar and makes it possible to change pitch without changing the fret position of the finger.

To bend a string follow these steps:
- Depress the string with the left-hand finger.
- Maintain pressure as you push the string upward or pull it downward.

Bends are indicated in the music by a curved or pointed slur (∧) in standard notation and an arrow in tablature. Bending strings works best on steel-string guitars and is done most easily on light gauge strings with an unwound third string.

Below are some characteristic bends.

TRACK 10

THE DOUBLE STOP

A **double stop** is two notes played at once. Guitarists such as Chuck Berry, Jimi Hendrix, Freddie King, and many others have used double stops to enhance their solos and fills.

Below are some characteristic double stops.

TRACK 11

THE SLIDE

A **slide** is a common left-hand technique that is used by blues guitarists to produce a smooth, flowing sound.

To perform a slide follow these steps:
- Depress the string with the left-hand finger.
- Pick the string with the right hand.
- Maintain pressure as you move your left-hand finger up or down the fretboard to the second position shown.

Below are some characteristic slides:

TRACK 12

One of the all-time Chicago blues legends, Howlin Wolf (Chester Burnett), wrote the classic "Sitting on Top of the World." In this arrangement, we're going to touch on a lot of things that will help push your blues guitar knowledge to the next level. It's a blues in the key of A in which the IV chord goes to minor, and for extra fun, I've included the "hook" of the tune, using quarter step-bends, double stops, and slides. Don't be afraid. These nuances are standard blues fare, and the sooner we tackle them the better. First, let's take a look at the A blues scale in open position.

The A Blues Scale

Visualize this box shape as it relates to the A chord because this association will come in handy as we take the A-string-rooted blues tunes, and move them up and down the neck.

TRACK 13

SITTING ON TOP OF THE WORLD

THE MAJOR PENTATONIC SCALE

In measure 2 of the previous song, there are two slides that achieve a slurring effect by picking the first note and quickly sliding up with the same finger immediately following the initial stroke. You may notice that the notes used in the slide aren't necessarily in the blues scale. The **major pentatonic scale** (root–2nd–3rd–5th–6th) is the partner to the blues scale for improvisation in the blues. Here is the A major pentatonic scale in this position.

A Major Pentatonic

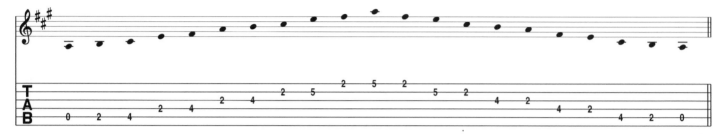

THE PULL-OFF

Another typical blues technique is the **pull-off**. The pull-off is named for the action of the left-hand fingers on the fretboard.

To perform a pull-off follow these steps:
- Depress the string with the left-hand finger.
- Pick the string with the right hand.
- Maintain pressure as you pull the left-hand finger toward the palm of your hand to sound the note behind it on the same string, using the initial attack to carry the tone.

Below are some characteristic pull-offs:

TRACK 14

First, the legendary Buddy Guy, and then the mighty Stevie Ray Vaughan have taken the classic nursery rhyme "Mary Had a Little Lamb" from the pages of children's books to the land of the blues. This arrangement is a good exercise of bouncing between fills and a chordal rhythm patterns in open position. There are also some new things to add to your ever-increasing blues guitar vocabulary. In measure 10, notice the pull-off on the second beat of the triplet. On beats 3–4 of measure 4, there is the return of the major pentatonic scale, this time in E. Here is the E major pentatonic zone to aim for in this position.

E Major Pentatonic

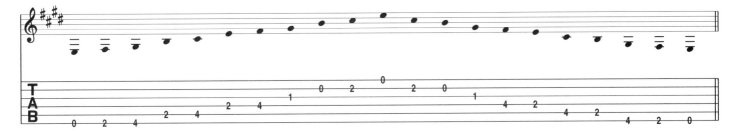

As you play through this arrangement, try the suggested strumming patterns for best results.

TRACK 15

MARY HAD A LITTLE LAMB

Medium Blues

VIBRATO

One of the most emotive and widely used techniques of blues guitar is **vibrato**. It can be either a shallow, quick quiver or a wide, succulent, earth-shaking move. Vibrato is achieved by pushing and pulling the string up and down with your fret hand after sounding a note. This gives the note a more "singing" quality.

Blues guitarists apply vibrato as follows:
- Depress the string with the left-hand finger.
- Pick the string with the right hand.
- Maintain pressure as you push and pull the string perpendicular to its length.

Vibrato is indicated in music by a wavy line above standard notation and tablature:

TRACK 16

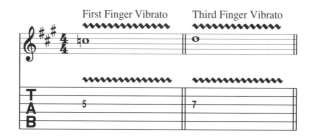

Experiment with the width of the vibrato. Some players prefer a slow, wide vibrato; others favor a fast, shallow vibrato.

B. B. King is famous for his version of the **pivot vibrato**, known as the "butterfly" vibrato. The technique gets its name from the visual effect created when B.B. vibratoes notes with his index finger while fanning out the remaining fingers. The resulting sound is a tight, rapidly fluctuating vibrato. It helps to anchor your thumb at the top of the fretboard to provide counterforce, and by rotating your arm back and forth about its long axis, the pitch of the note is raised by slightly bending the string and then releasing it.

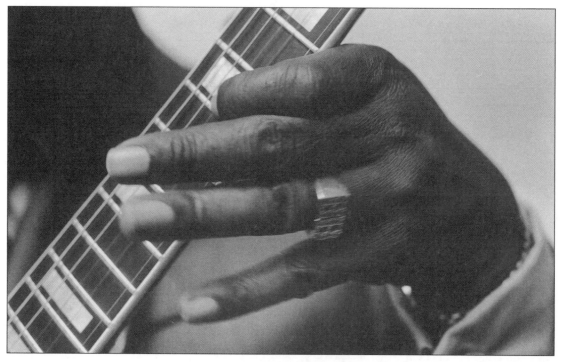

B.B. King "Butterfly" Vibrato

The following arrangement of Muddy Waters' "I Can't Be Satisfied" provides you the opportunity to apply some introductory vibrato, as well as a new root/5th bass pattern and another movable turnaround.

The tune opens with a double stop that includes a slide or a bend up to a unison. This is a widely used technique in blues and rock guitar. Be sure to let those notes ring out! Next, you get your chance to ply your vibrato to the A note at the second fret. Try using a medium-size vibrato to start. Eventually, however, we're going to want that note to sting a little, so once you're comfortable with the basic technique, get under it with your second finger and make it sound like you mean it! When playing the alternating root/5th bass pattern, try choking the chords with your right-hand palm to add a more percussive feel. The turn-around on this tune is a blues classic. It is most easily played if you try to develop either a pick and finger technique or play it thumb and fingerstyle to most effectively address the string skipping between the notes of the triplets in measure 11.

TRACK 17

I CAN'T BE SATISFIED

OPEN-POSITION SHUFFLE PATTERNS

The following rhythm patterns are widely used by all blues guitarists, from Jimmy Reed to Stevie Ray Vaughan. Try alternating between all downstrokes with your strumming hand, and accenting the off-beats with an upstroke.

Shuffle in E

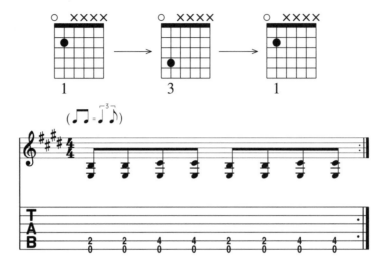

Shuffle in A

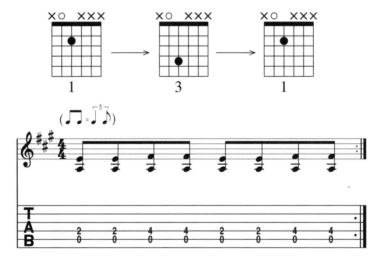

Shuffle in D

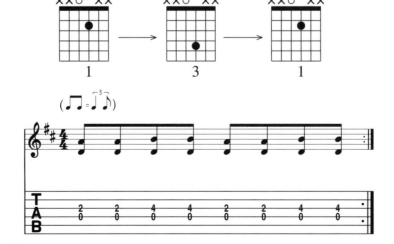

Stevie Ray's "Look at Little Sister" utilizes the open-position shuffle pattern you just learned. Note that Stevie uses a variation of the shuffle pattern that has the A string ringing out even when you're on the V (B) chord. Jimmy Reed and others used to do this to bring the tension to the boiling point. Remember: choke the chords on the downbeat with you right-hand palm.

TRACK 21

LOOK AT LITTLE SISTER

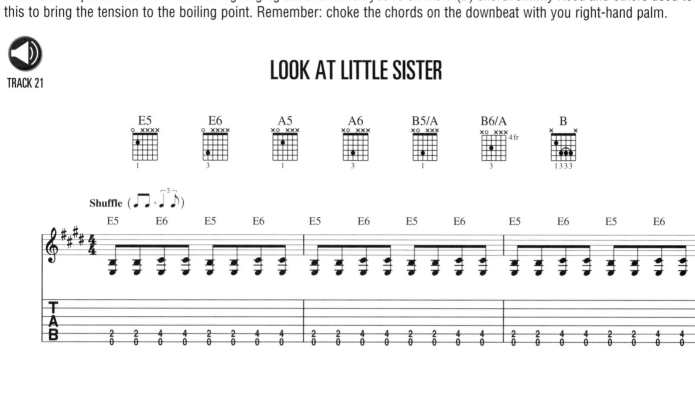

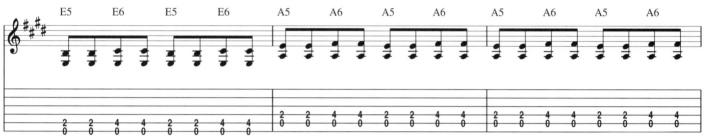

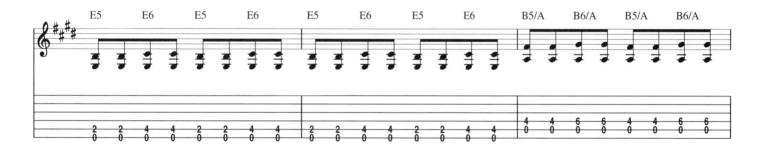

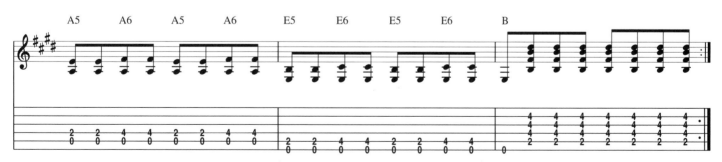

THE EXTENDED BLUES SCALE

Using the slow-tempo, Willie Dixon-meets-Led Zeppelin tune "You Shook Me" as an example, we will now further examine the shuffle pattern, add a new turnaround, continue with vibrato, introduce hammer-ons, and extend our E blues scale in open position. Let's begin with the extended E blues scale.

Extending the E blues scale in this position is, again, something that will be very useful as we start to move these shapes up the neck. Having that visual association with the scale and root chord position of the blues progression will help you establish target areas to improvise until your ears take over. This extension establishes a "zone" with which you should become familiar.

Extended E Blues Scale

THE HAMMER-ON

The **hammer-on** is the opposite of the pull-off. To perform a hammer-on follow these steps:
- Depress the string with the left-hand finger.
- Pick the string with the right hand.
- Maintain pressure as you quickly press down onto the fret of the second (higher) note on the same string, using the initial attack to carry the tone.

Below are some characteristic hammer-ons:

TRACK 22

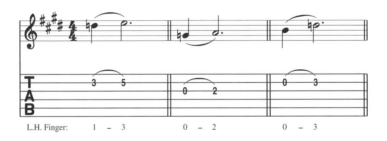

Now, let's take an in-depth look at "You Shook Me" (see next page). The hook of this tune, which starts with the pickup measure, has a quarter-step bend on the G note to add a slurring effect. As you are in the extended zone of the E blues scale, this bend is done with your first finger and requires a slight, pushing up of the high E string. The vibrato indicated is going to be done with your third finger, and you're going to rock the B string up and down to achieve a "singing effect," which should be your goal when applying a vibrato.

Skipping ahead to measure 11, you'll see a hammer-on on the "and" of beat 4. This particular hammer-on is a good blues example because after picking the open G note (minor 3rd) you are quickly hammering onto the G# note (major 3rd) using the initial stroke to sustain the note. This minor-to-major 3rd move is often used when soloing in the blues scale (which does not include a major 3rd) because the I chord, or E in this case, does contain the major 3rd.

The turnaround in this arrangement (measure 12) can either be strummed or played with a combination of pick and fingers or thumb and fingers. That option is up to you, but I recommend experimenting with each of these techniques.

Now that we have established some zones for improvising and have learned some nuances, let's jam over "You Shook Me." We'll play the arrangement twice, then it's time to burn! Experiment with the extended E blues scale and the E major pentatonic scale we learned on "Mary Had a Little Lamb." Also, try squeezing in a couple of the turnarounds that we've learned thus far.

YOU SHOOK ME

HARMONIZED SHUFFLE PATTERNS

A great way to create harmonic movement and excitement in your blues rhythms is to harmonize the chords. In the next example, I've illustrated harmonized shuffle patterns for the most popular chords used in open-position blues: E, A, D, and G.

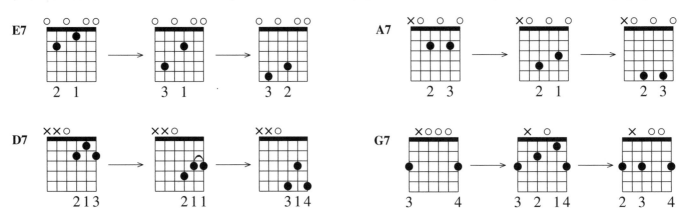

The following example of a harmonized shuffle in D utilizes the D, G, and A versions of these chord progressions as well as another chordal turnaround for your blues arsenal. There's another new technique introduced here, too: the open-string upbeat. In an eighth-note shuffle groove, especially when changing chord voicings, it helps to have time for your frethand fingers to move to the next chord without losing the groove. By strumming strings 2, 3, and 4 open—or slightly muted—on the upbeat, your fingers will be in position to play on the next downbeat.

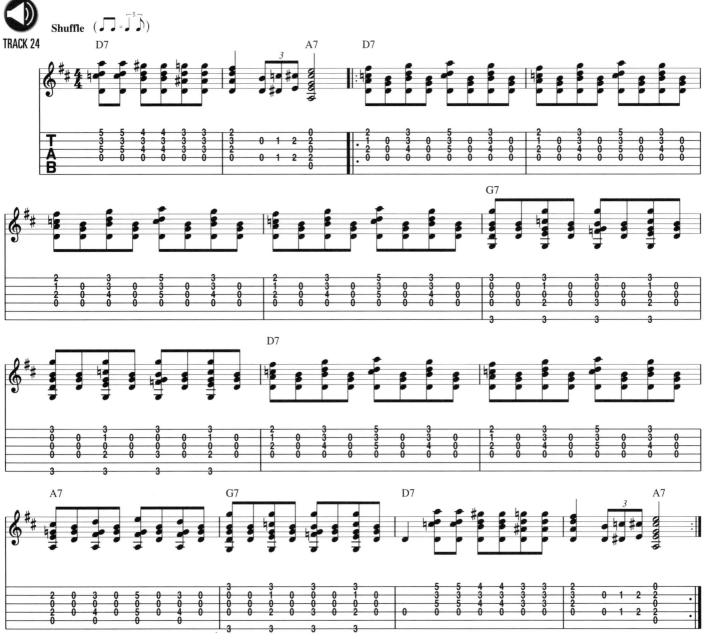

Now, let's integrate the harmonized shuffle into a true blues classic: "Ramblin' on My Mind" by Robert Johnson. This slow blues arrangement combines a harmonized shuffle pattern with some classic blues fills and a new single-note turnaround. The fills in measures 6 and 7 use hammer-ons to again emphasize the major third of the E (I) chord. Both the turnaround/intro and the aforementioned fills include some chromatic notes that come from neither the blues nor major pentatonic scales. This is a very cool effect for improvising. Also in the turnaround/intro, the ending B7 chord has the fifth (F#) in the bass. This is a commonly used inversion of the V chord in blues, especially in the key of E based in open position.

TRACK 25

RAMBLIN' ON MY MIND

BOOGIE PATTERNS

In rounding out our study of blues in open and first position, let's take a look at some repeating boogie patterns that have been used by every blues artist ever to walk. These are a terrific departure from using normal chord voicings in the blues form as they provide an upbeat sense of forward motion. Use alternate picking as you play through these exercises at different tempos.

TRACK 26

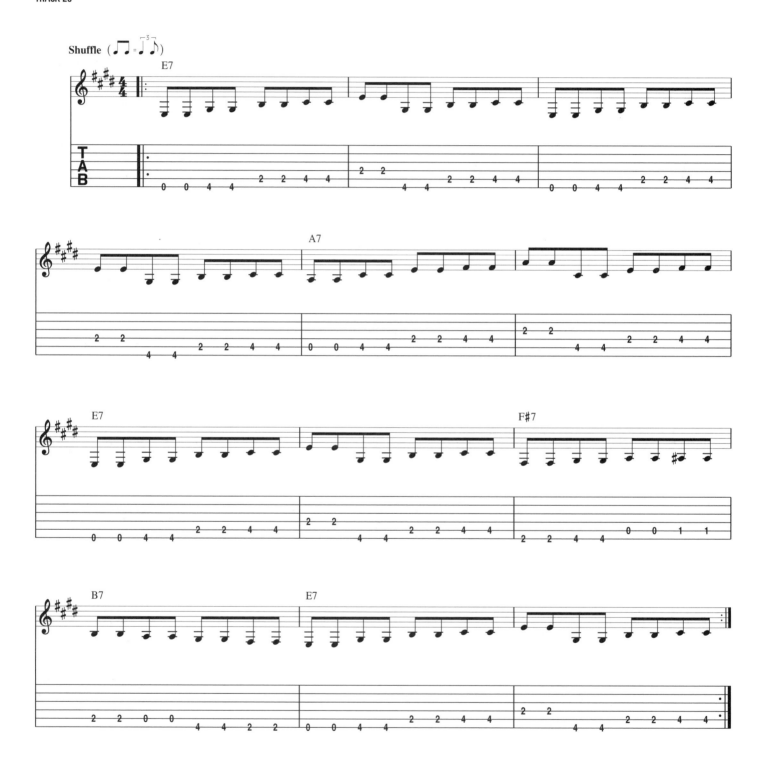

MOVABLE PATTERNS

You may have noticed that we've spent a lot of time in the keys of E and A up until this point. This is not just because they're popular blues keys; it's because the chord shapes and scale positions are movable and therefore can be played anywhere on the neck. This brings us to our next section: Movable patterns.

All of our hard work in first position is now going to pay off as we venture up the neck of the guitar. One of the easiest ways to get a grasp on playing the blues in various keys is to find the root of the new key on either the E or A string and play the same scale and chord patterns from that root that you used to play the blues in open position. By using your index finger as a makeshift capo, the open-position shuffle patterns you learned earlier become movable patterns.

Hand position for movable shuffle pattern

TRACK 28
Shuffle in G

TRACK 29
Shuffle in C

Chords are named after the position of the first finger on each pattern. In the key of F, place your first finger on fret 1 of string 6. In the key of D, place your first finger on fret 5 of string 5, and so on.

EXTENDED CHORDS

Movable 9th Chord Shape

2 1 3 3 3

In addition to creating movable patterns out of open-position chords and scales, it's time to learn a new type of chord: the extended chord. Extended chords have names that end in 9th, 11th, or 13th. Here is the chord diagram for the most popular extended chord in the blues genre: the ninth chord with the root in the bass.

Let's take a moment to explain how you come up with terms like 9th, 11th, and 13th. If you'll recall, we've already stacked notes on top of our triad to get seventh chords at the start of this book. If we stack another third on top of that, in this next example an E note on a D7 chord, we get a ninth, or a D9. If we stack another third, it's the 11th, then the 13th.

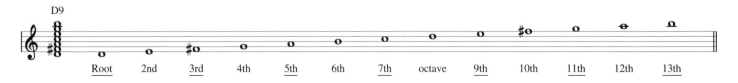

These notes are the same as the 2nd, 4th, and 6th in relation to the root note, but an octave higher in pitch. It's just a matter of counting, so don't let it rattle you!

Now, let's see how these movable patterns and extended chords can be used in a song. "Blow, Wind, Blow" is an uptempo shuffle by Muddy Waters in the key of G. This arrangement uses the movable shuffle pattern in G and includes a sliding seventh-chord fill as part of the tune's hook. Also included is a new, movable turnaround as well as a couple of ninth chords at the very end.

To solo over this tune, you'll need to use the G blues scale. Take a moment to review the movable blues scale box pattern in G, as well as the extended G blues scale.

We'll play the arrangement as written twice. Then, play a solo using the blues scale in the key of G. Try to incorporate some of the techniques, such as vibrato, hammer-ons and pull-offs, and double stops, that you learned in open position.

TRACK 30

BLOW, WIND, BLOW

Written by Muddy Waters
© 1969 (Renewed 1997) WATERTOONS MUSIC (BMI)/Administered by BUG MUSIC
All Rights Reserved   Used by Permission

MOVABLE SEVENTH CHORDS

Just like moving our shuffle pattern, we can also move our seventh chords from open position up the neck by using the first finger to make barre chords. The following two examples are the movable E7 and A7 shapes and are the most widely used.

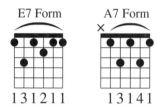

Note that on the A7 version of this barre chord, I have only indicated that the first finger barre from the A string up to the high E string, instead of barring all the strings including the low E. This is because the root of the chord is on the A string.

Let's plug these new chord shapes into the Robert Johnson classic, "I Believe I'll Dust My Broom" (see next page). From Johnson to Elmore James to ZZ Top, just about every blues band has at one time or another played a version of the uptempo shuffle. This particular arrangement in the key of D uses the movable shuffle rhythm pattern combined with the chordal hook of the song and a double-stop bend and vibrato.

Right from the beginning, the hook starts with a D major chord shape at the tenth fret that can be strummed in an alternate picking manner or with all down strokes for effect. The double-stop bend in bar 2, can be pulled up or down to achieve the quarter-step bend but the vibrato that immediately follows on the D string at the 12th fret is most easily done by pulling the string slightly down first, and then rocking it in and out of pitch from the original note. On the D string, you can get more authority in your vibrato by doing this.

The turnaround in measures 11 and 12 gives us a another variation and uses the movable E7 and A7 barre chord shapes.

For soloing on "I Believe I'll Dust My Broom," you can use the movable blues scale pattern at the tenth fret.

D Blues Scale - 10th fret

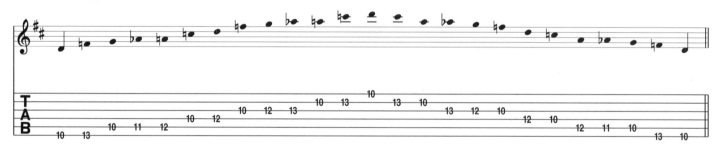

Let's also look, however, at the blues scale form at the fifth fret. The pattern is the same as what we learned as the A blues scale in open position, but it's now moved up the neck to the key of D, or the fifth fret. Go back over the form and practice using this new scale pattern in your solo.

D Blues Scale - 5th fret

I BELIEVE I'LL DUST MY BROOM

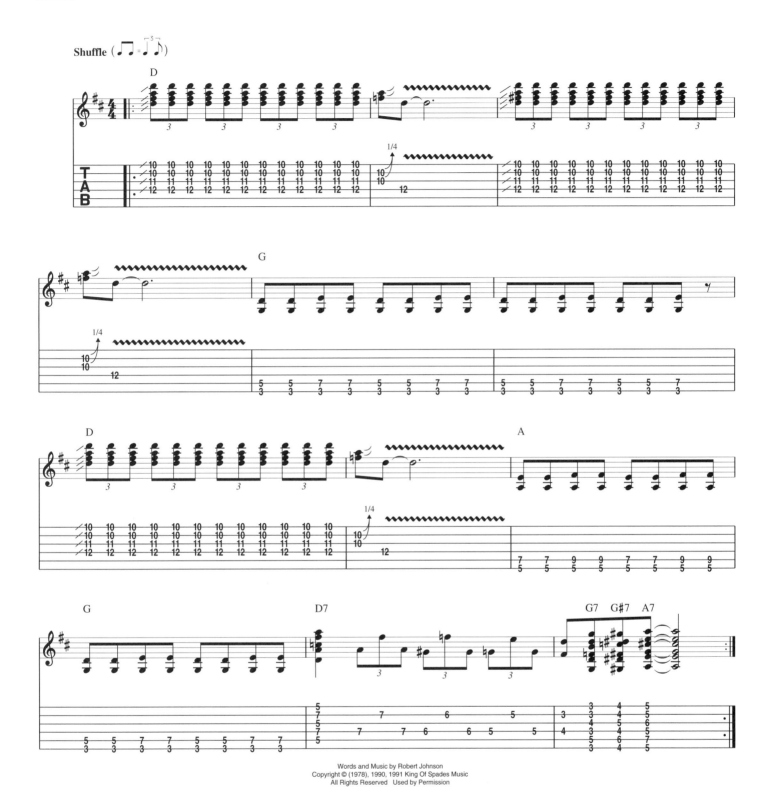

THE STYLE OF HOWLIN' WOLF

Let's go back to the topic of rhythm guitar for a moment. The ability to bounce back and forth between single notes and chords is a requisite talent for the aspiring blues guitarist. This concept is very well demonstrated in the Howlin Wolf's high-energy, uptempo, funky blues masterpiece, "Killing Floor." The repeating bass line is accented by a couple of seventh-chord blasts at the beginning of each bar. Use alternate picking on the single notes and apply a slight palm mute with your picking hand.

TRACK 32

KILLING FLOOR

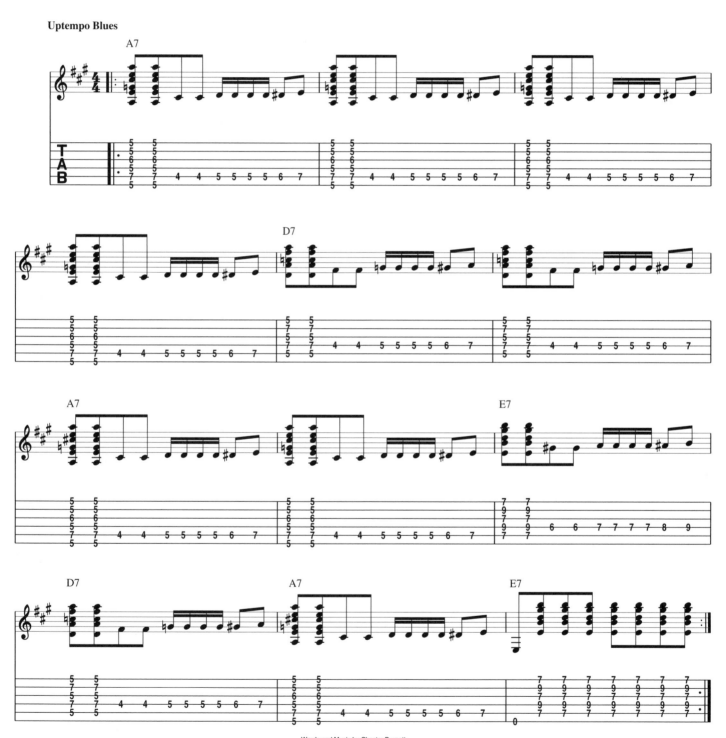

Words and Music by Chester Burnett
Copyright © 1965, 1970 (Renewed) by Arc Music Corporation (BMI)
International Copyright Secured   All Rights Reserved   Used by Permission

THE STYLE OF B.B. KING

Examining the style of the "King of the Blues," B.B. King, is a must for any budding blues guitarist. Some of the keys to B.B.'s trademark sound are his note choices, his vibrato, and his string-bending. Let's first talk about note choice. The following diagram shows a small grouping of notes that are taken from both the major pentatonic and blues scales. We'll call this the "B.B. Zone."

B.B.'s played entire solos using just these six notes. It just goes to show how true the old adage is—sometimes less really is more!

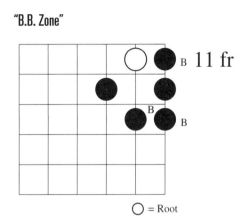

"B.B. Zone"

○ = Root

Now, let's discuss the second key: vibrato. The root (B♭) in this example is a note that B.B. often grinds into the fretboard with his singing vibrato. As discussed earlier on page 16, this is best achieved by shaking the note back and forth quickly from your wrist as you literally grind the string into the fretboard with your first finger.

The next key is string-bending. The following licks introduce half- and full-step bends in the "B.B. Zone." The key to good bending is achieving the proper pitch. The easiest way to train your ear to recognize this is by first fretting the note up to which you wish to bend the string. For example, in Lick 1, the C note at the thirteenth fret gets bent one half step to D♭. To be sure you're getting to the right pitch, first play the D♭ note at the 14th fret, then play the C note at the 13th fret and bend the string until the pitch matches the D♭ you just played. Do this as often as necessary until your ear can reliably hear half- and full-step bends. Don't be discouraged; with practice, you'll get it. Other notes that are bent regularly in this zone are indicated with the letter B in the diagram above.

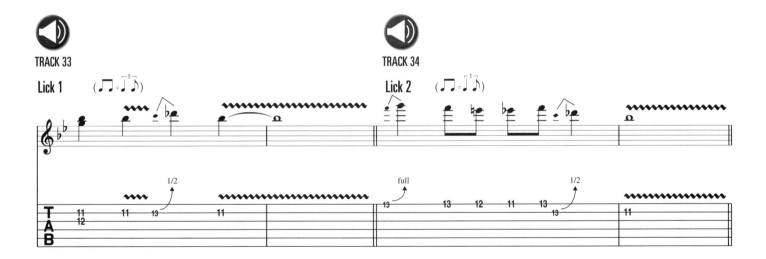

TRACK 33

Lick 1

TRACK 34

Lick 2

Following is an arrangement of King's "Rock Me Baby" in B♭. It features a movable, sliding ninth chord—a fave of B.B.'s and one of the most commonly heard motifs in the blues genre. We'll play through the song form twice, and then it's time to solo. Try using the "B.B. Zone" as well as licks 1 and 2 and the other soloing tools you've learned thus far. Here we go!

ROCK ME BABY

TRACK 35

THE STYLE OF ALBERT KING

Another "King of the Blues" whom every blues guitarist should study is the mighty Albert King. A word of caution, however: the lead guitar style of Albert King can be quite trying because it incorporates a lot of huge bends. These callus-busters, however, were no problem for him because he had huge, powerful hands, plus he played left-handed with the strings upside-down, so he pulled them down instead of pushing them up. You might want to consider starting with a lighter set of strings if you're really into Albert's style and want to play a lot of his tunes.

In terms of note choice, Albert stayed in the minor pentatonic scale most of the time and squeezed just what he needed out of those five notes. In fact, like B.B. King (no relation), Albert spent a large portion of his soloing time in the extended pattern of the minor pentatonic scale—a pattern that has come to be known as the "Albert King box." The minor pentatonic scale (root, ♭3rd, 4th, 5th, ♭7th) is the same as the blues scale minus the flatted fifth "blues note."

C♯ Minor Pentatonic Scale

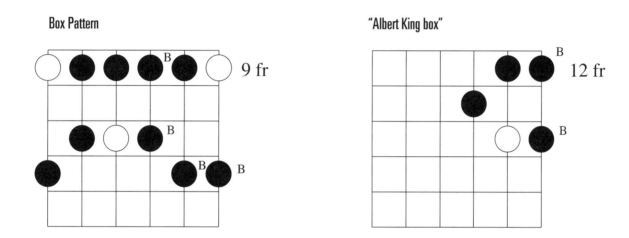

Box Pattern

"Albert King box"

Here are two licks that offer a glimpse into the style of the master. The first is based in the box pattern and contains a whole-step bend to which you add vibrato once you reach the top of the bend. This is very difficult at first, but as you strengthen your fingers, you can really pay attention to your vibrato, which, in Albert's case, is wide and buttery. The second lick is based in the Albert King box and has a whole-step bend on the E string that can really be accented by popping the note with your index finger on the attack.

Albert King Licks

Lick 1   TRACK 36

Lick 2   TRACK 37

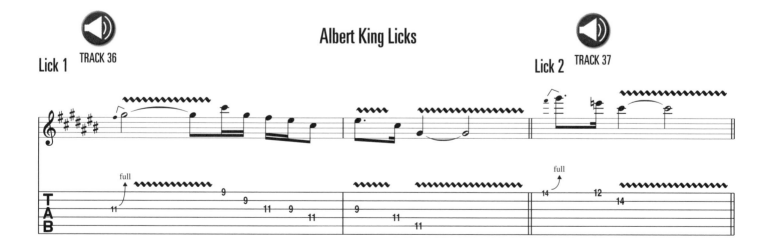

Albert King's version of "Born Under a Bad Sign" has become a blues standard. It features a bass line-like guitar riff that is repeated throughout, fun to play, and sounds great. Like "Killing Floor," we will again bounce between single notes and seventh chords to play this arrangement. Use the C# minor pentatonic scale for your solo and concentrate on bending on the notes indicated with the letter B in the diagrams on the previous page. Keep in mind that you can bend any note that you want as long as it sounds good but the ones indicated are the most common notes to bend up a half or whole step.

TRACK 38

BORN UNDER A BAD SIGN

THE STYLE OF T-BONE WALKER

T-Bone Walker is widely considered the father of electric blues guitar. From Bobby Bland to the Allman Brothers Band to T-Bone Walker himself, the keys and chords used to play "(They Call It) Stormy Monday (Stormy Monday Blues)" vary widely throughout the different renditions of the tune. The arrangement presented here reflects various aspects taken from these many versions of his famous slow blues. It starts with a classic T-Bone Walker lick that uses one of our seventh chord voicings and bends the notes a quarter step. Then, many new chord voicings are introduced that can be used in place of or in addition to the other chord shapes now in your rhythm guitar bag of tricks. Practice these new chords and then use them in the following arrangement.

TRACK 39

(THEY CALL IT) STORMY MONDAY (STORMY MONDAY BLUES)

THE STYLE OF FREDDIE KING

No blues guitar book would be complete without touching on the style of the third "King of the Blues," Freddie King. On Freddie's "I'm Tore Down," we have a repeating line for which you can substitute, or embellish with, any of the seventh or ninth chords you've learned up to this point. This arrangement features the signature single-note shuffle pattern in the key of C that can be played either slightly muted or allowed to ring out loud and proud.

When you're ready to solo on this song, try using this new version of the blues scale.

Modified C Blues Scale

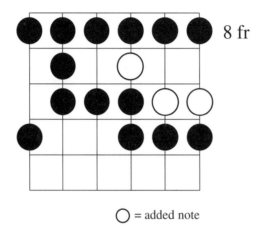

8 fr

○ = added note

Here, we've borrowed a few notes from the major pentatonic scale to add a little Freddie King flavor to the "blues zone" that we've been using thus far. The following two licks use notes from this new hybrid scale. In the first, a triplet leads into a whole-step bend in the "added note" area of our blues scale. Though it's basically a major pentatonic lick, it might be less confusing if you look at it as adding notes to what you already know. The second lick has a little more meat and is also triplet-driven. This is a good example of the Freddie King style.

Freddie King Licks

Lick 1 TRACK 40   **Lick 2** TRACK 41

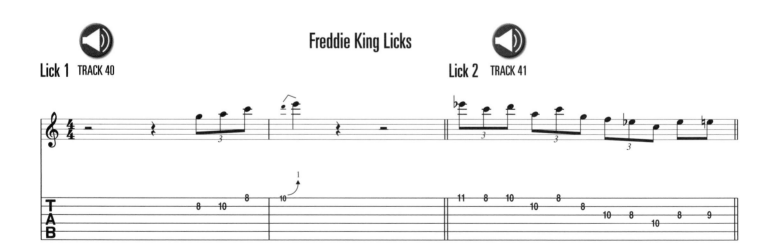

Now, let's pull all of these elements together and "tear down" this shuffle in C.

TRACK 42

I'M TORE DOWN

Intro

Verse

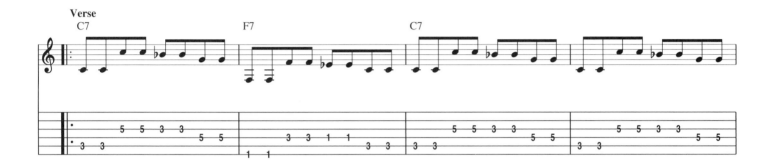

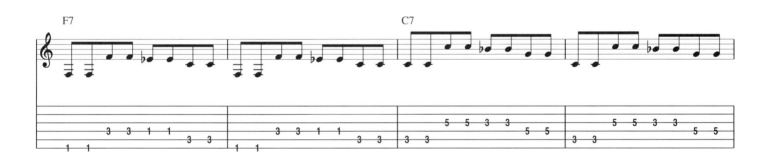

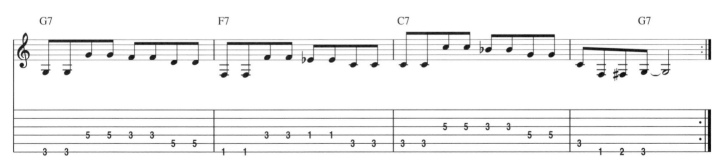

REPEATING RIFF BLUES

Some blues tunes never stray from the I chord and just repeat a riff or a lick over and over again. Howlin Wolf's "I'm Leavin' You (Commit a Crime)," which was also done by Stevie Ray Vaughan, is a good example of this strategy, as is John Lee Hooker's classic, "Boom Boom."

I'M LEAVIN' YOU (COMMIT A CRIME)

Words and Music by Chester Burnett
Copyright © 1960 (Renewed) by Arc Music Corporation (BMI)
International Copyright Secured   All Rights Reserved   Used by Permission

BOOM BOOM

Words and Music by John Lee Hooker
Copyright © 1962, 1965 (Renewed) by Conrad Music, a division of Arc Music Corp. (BMI)
International Copyright Secured   All Rights Reserved   Used by Permission

Another great example of the I chord vamp is Muddy Water's "Mannish Boy." This timeless riff is written in a 12/8 time signature. This means that there are 12 eighth notes in each measure. The 12/8 time signature has a triplet feel, so you can think of it as 4/4 time with eighth-note triplets. This is a very common meter for the blues—especially slow blues.

MANNISH BOY

Words and Music by McKinley Morganfield (Muddy Waters), M.R. London and Ellas McDaniel
Copyright © 1955 (Renewed) by Arc Music Corporation (BMI), Lonmel Publishing (BMI) and Watertoons Music (BMI)/Administered by Bug Music
International Copyright Secured   All Rights Reserved   Used by Permission

MINOR BLUES

Slow blues tunes are often played in a minor key, thus creating what is commonly known as a **minor blues**. Such is the case with our next song, "Double Trouble," written by the highly influential Otis Rush.

Following is a typical minor blues progression:

TRACK 46

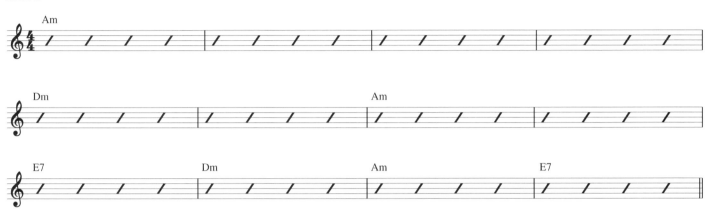

The progression used in "Double Trouble" is a variation of the example above. It substitutes minor seventh chords for minor chords and stays on the "one" chord in measures 11 and 12.

"Double Trouble" also introduces a new blues technique: combining rhythm and lead guitar into one part. The most challenging part of this arrangement is the quick, whole-step bend as found in the pickup measure and measure 2. A combination of pick-hand muting and a slight release of the string with your fret hand will "choke" the note so it doesn't ring into the next portion of the beat.

When it comes time to solo, you can stick to the notes of the B blues scale over each chord and not worry about hitting wrong notes. For some added spice, however, play the blues scale of each chord in the progression. That is, play the B blues scale over the Bm7 chord, the E blues scale over the Em7 chord, and the F#m blues scale over the F#m7 chord.

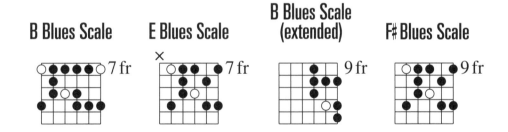

DOUBLE TROUBLE

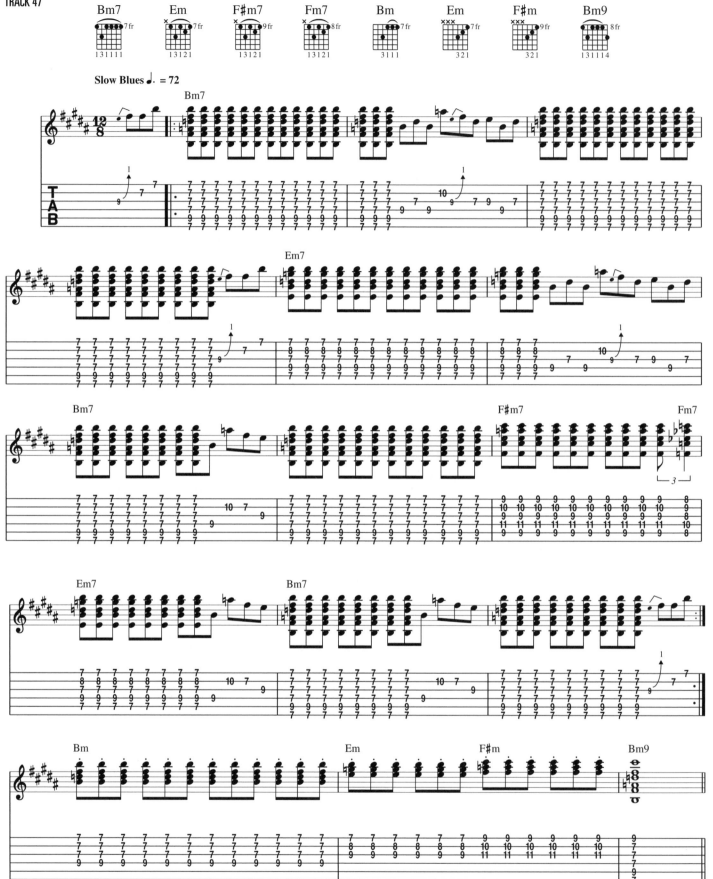

PUTTING IT ALL TOGETHER

Now it's time to take what you've learned so far and play along with the jam tracks. Practice the chords for each of the following seven blues progressions, then try soloing. Use the licks at the bottom of the page as the basis for your solos. You may also use licks you learned earlier, or try coming up with a few of your own.

MEDIUM SHUFFLE BLUES

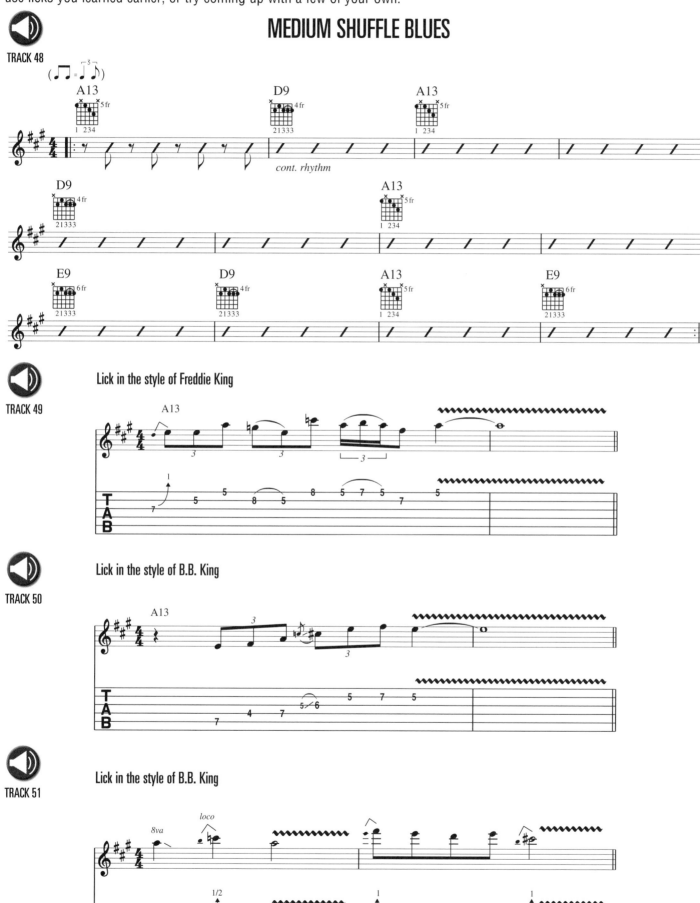

TRACK 48

TRACK 49 — Lick in the style of Freddie King

TRACK 50 — Lick in the style of B.B. King

TRACK 51 — Lick in the style of B.B. King

TRACK 52

TRACK 53

Lick in the style of Albert Collins

TRACK 54

Lick in the style of Stevie Ray Vaughan

TRACK 55

Lick in the style of Jimmie Vaughan

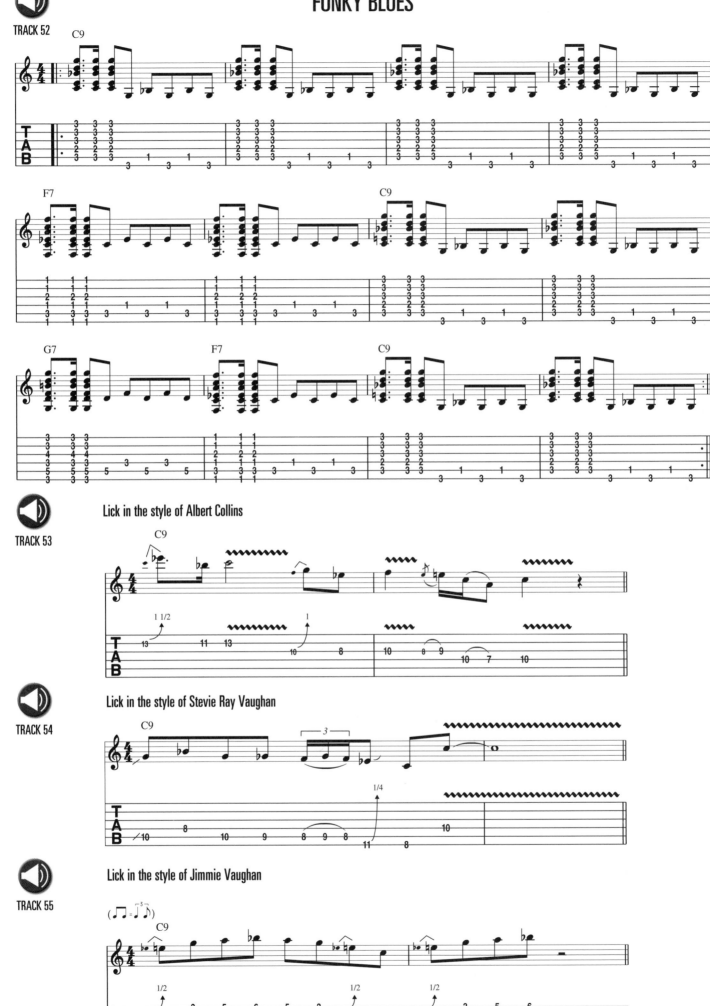

SLOW MINOR BLUES

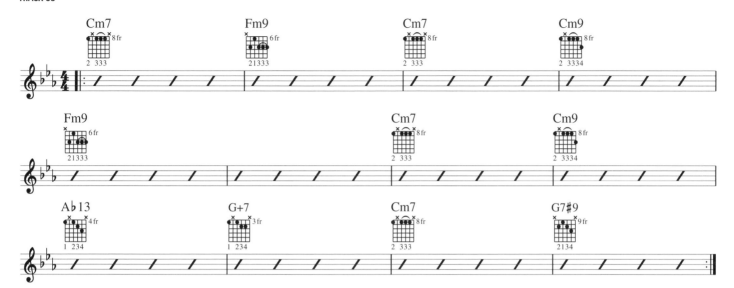

Lick in the style of B.B. King

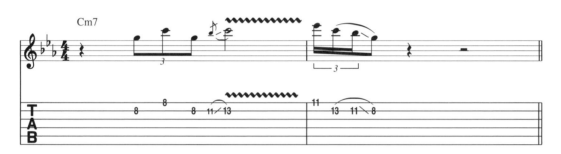

Lick in the style of Billy Gibbons

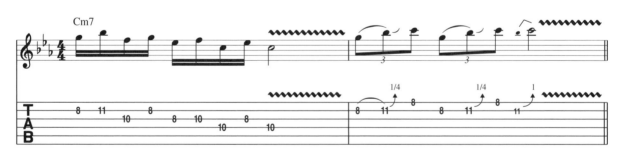

Lick in the style of Eric Clapton

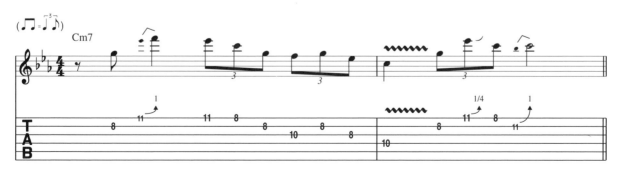

RHUMBA BLUES

TRACK 60

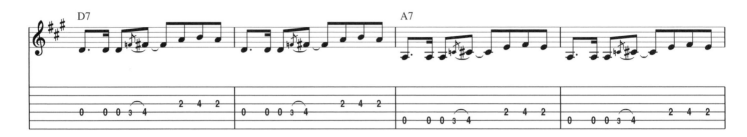

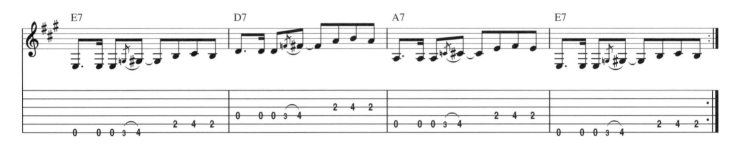

TRACK 61

Lick in the style of Albert King

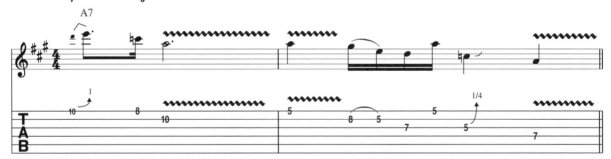

TRACK 62

Lick in the style of Jimi Hendrix

TRACK 63

Lick in the style of Dickey Betts

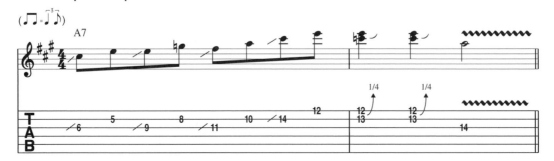

SLOW SHUFFLE BLUES

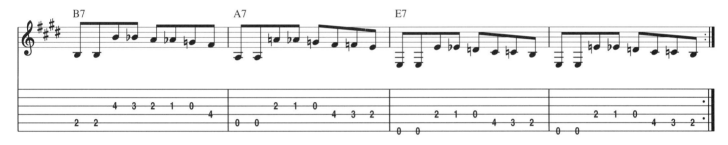

Lick in the style of Stevie Ray Vaughan

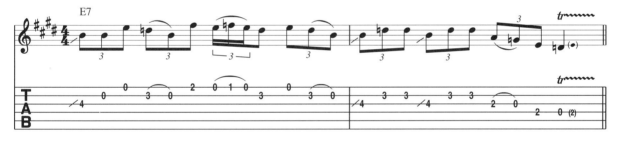

Lick in the style of Buddy Guy

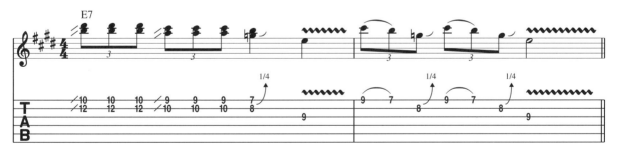

Lick in the style of Eric Clapton

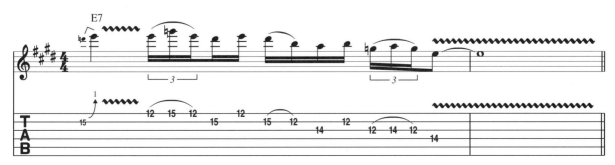

TRACK 68

SLOW BLUES/JAZZ

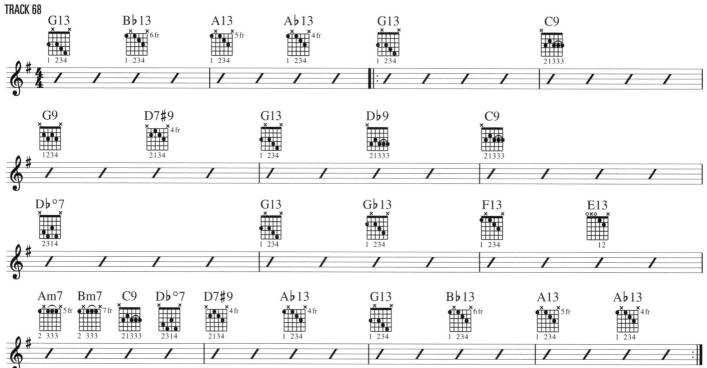

TRACK 69

Lick in the style of T-Bone Walker

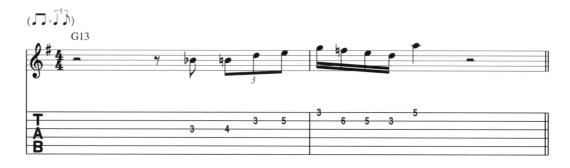

TRACK 70

Lick in the style of B.B. King

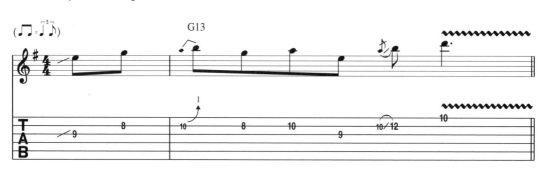

TRACK 71

Lick in the style of B.B. King

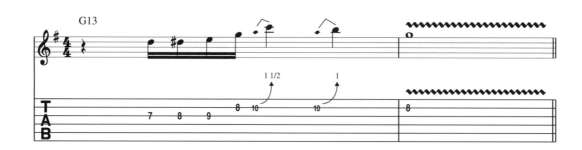

SWING BLUES

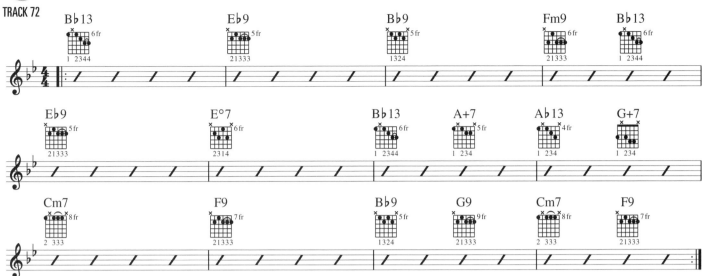

Lick in the style of T-Bone Walker

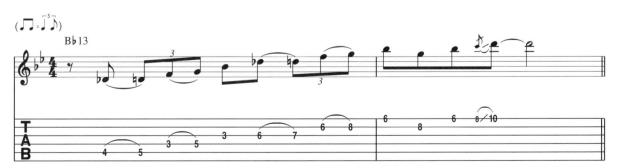

Lick in the style of T-Bone Walker

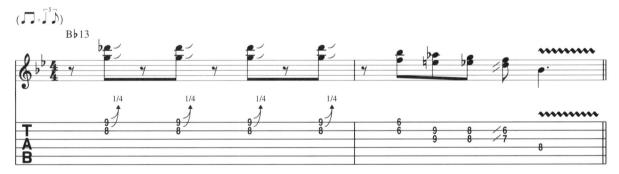

Lick in the style of Charlie Christian

HAL LEONARD GUITAR METHOD

METHOD BOOKS, SONGBOOKS AND REFERENCE BOOKS

HAL LEONARD GUITAR METHOD BOOK 1
SECOND EDITION
INCLUDES CD AND ONLINE AUDIO ACCESS
BY WILL SCHMID AND GREG KOCH

THE HAL LEONARD GUITAR METHOD is designed for anyone just learning to play acoustic or electric guitar. It is based on years of teaching guitar students of all ages, and it also reflects some of the best guitar teaching ideas from around the world. This comprehensive method includes: A learning sequence carefully paced with clear instructions; popular songs which increase the incentive to learn to play; versatility – can be used as self-instruction or with a teacher; audio accompaniments so that students have fun and sound great while practicing.

BOOK 1
00699010	Book Only	$8.99
00699027	Book/Online Audio	$12.99
00697341	Book/Online Audio + DVD	$24.99
00697318	DVD Only	$19.99
00155480	Deluxe Beginner Edition (Book, CD, DVD, Online Audio/ Video & Chord Poster)	$19.99

COMPLETE (BOOKS 1, 2 & 3)
00699040	Book Only	$16.99
00697342	Book/Online Audio	$24.99

BOOK 2
00699020	Book Only	$8.99
00697313	Book/Online Audio	$12.99

BOOK 3
00699030	Book Only	$8.99
00697316	Book/Online Audio	$12.99

Prices, contents and availability subject to change without notice.

STYLISTIC METHODS

ACOUSTIC GUITAR
00697347	Method Book/Online Audio	$17.99
00237969	Songbook/Online Audio	$16.99

BLUEGRASS GUITAR
00697405	Method Book/Online Audio	$16.99

BLUES GUITAR
00697326	Method Book/Online Audio (9" x 12")	$16.99
00697344	Method Book/Online Audio (6" x 9")	$15.99
00697385	Songbook/Online Audio (9" x 12")	$14.99
00248636	Kids Method Book/Online Audio	$12.99

BRAZILIAN GUITAR
00697415	Method Book/Online Audio	$17.99

CHRISTIAN GUITAR
00695947	Method Book/Online Audio	$16.99
00697408	Songbook/CD Pack	$14.99

CLASSICAL GUITAR
00697376	Method Book/Online Audio	$15.99

COUNTRY GUITAR
00697337	Method Book/Online Audio	$22.99
00697400	Songbook/Online Audio	$19.99

FINGERSTYLE GUITAR
00697378	Method Book/Online Audio	$21.99
00697432	Songbook/Online Audio	$16.99

FLAMENCO GUITAR
00697363	Method Book/Online Audio	$15.99

FOLK GUITAR
00697414	Method Book/Online Audio	$16.99

JAZZ GUITAR
00695359	Book/Online Audio	$22.99
00697386	Songbook/Online Audio	$15.99

JAZZ-ROCK FUSION
00697387	Book/Online Audio	$24.99

R&B GUITAR
00697356	Book/Online Audio	$19.99
00697433	Songbook/CD Pack	$14.99

ROCK GUITAR
00697319	Book/Online Audio	$16.99
00697383	Songbook/Online Audio	$16.99

ROCKABILLY GUITAR
00697407	Book/Online Audio	$16.99

OTHER METHOD BOOKS

BARITONE GUITAR METHOD
00242055	Book/Online Audio	$12.99

GUITAR FOR KIDS
00865003	Method Book 1/Online Audio	$12.99
00697402	Songbook/Online Audio	$9.99
00128437	Method Book 2/Online Audio	$12.99

MUSIC THEORY FOR GUITARISTS
00695790	Book/Online Audio	$19.99

TENOR GUITAR METHOD
00148330	Book/Online Audio	$12.99

12-STRING GUITAR METHOD
00249528	Book/Online Audio	$19.99

METHOD SUPPLEMENTS

ARPEGGIO FINDER
00697352	6" x 9" Edition	$6.99
00697351	9" x 12" Edition	$9.99

BARRE CHORDS
00697406	Book/Online Audio	$14.99

CHORD, SCALE & ARPEGGIO FINDER
00697410	Book Only	$19.99

GUITAR TECHNIQUES
00697389	Book/Online Audio	$16.99

INCREDIBLE CHORD FINDER
00697200	6" x 9" Edition	$7.99
00697208	9" x 12" Edition	$7.99

INCREDIBLE SCALE FINDER
00695568	6" x 9" Edition	$9.99
00695490	9" x 12" Edition	$9.99

LEAD LICKS
00697345	Book/Online Audio	$10.99

RHYTHM RIFFS
00697346	Book/Online Audio	$14.99

SONGBOOKS

CLASSICAL GUITAR PIECES
00697388	Book/Online Audio	$9.99

EASY POP MELODIES
00697281	Book Only	$7.99
00697440	Book/Online Audio	$14.99

(MORE) EASY POP MELODIES
00697280	Book Only	$6.99
00697269	Book/Online Audio	$14.99

(EVEN MORE) EASY POP MELODIES
00699154	Book Only	$6.99
00697439	Book/Online Audio	$14.99

EASY POP RHYTHMS
00697336	Book Only	$7.99
00697441	Book/Online Audio	$14.99

(MORE) EASY POP RHYTHMS
00697338	Book Only	$7.99
00697322	Book/Online Audio	$14.99

(EVEN MORE) EASY POP RHYTHMS
00697340	Book Only	$7.99
00697323	Book/Online Audio	$14.99

EASY POP CHRISTMAS MELODIES
00697417	Book Only	$9.99
00697416	Book/Online Audio	$14.99

EASY POP CHRISTMAS RHYTHMS
00278177	Book Only	$6.99
00278175	Book/Online Audio	$14.99

EASY SOLO GUITAR PIECES
00110407	Book Only	$9.99

REFERENCE

GUITAR PRACTICE PLANNER
00697401	Book Only	$5.99

GUITAR SETUP & MAINTENANCE
00697427	6" x 9" Edition	$14.99
00697421	9" x 12" Edition	$12.99

For more info, songlists, or to purchase these and more books from your favorite music retailer, go to

halleonard.com

HAL•LEONARD®